THIRD EYE AWAKENING III

THERONE SHELLMAN

ISBN: 13-978-1722710958

Third Eye Awakening III Edited by Therone Shellman Media, Typeset by Therone Shellman Media, Proofread by Therone Shellman Media

CONTENTS

INTRODUCTION

The first two books from the Third Eye Awakening series, encompass, spiritual, mental health, the history of where modern religious beliefs come from, physical health and practices, self-development, and empowerment. Book III is about taking all of what you've learned within the first two books, and developing the necessary skills to explore what you're inspired to do.

As a teen, I thought about writing books. Yet I didn't see it as a business opportunity, because I just saw writers who wrote books, or for newspapers. It would be years later that the idea of writing books and entrepreneurship seemed like an achievable possibility, and I became open to the reality a lot of African Americans were in fact business owners. Growing up in Long Island, I wasn't exposed to the reality.

By my early twenties, entrepreneurism was deeply implanted in my psyche. But I was still somewhat crippled by my heredity and past social beliefs which I gained through others. I lacked financial literacy because I grew up poor and was taught to be poor. Without the necessary proper guidance, I made critical mistakes as a teen which would affect me for many years, over a decade to be exact. It would not be until I reached the Age of twenty-eight that I would find my life somewhat mentally free from turmoil to allow myself to begin to set a definite plan. Entrepreneurship is what keeps the economy and social systems of the world going. But the occupation entails so many skills which people lack and most are not willing to take the time to seek and learn.

For humans life is a process of self discovery. We can lose ourselves looking out into the physical world, seeking to find ourselves. Let's admit in all honesty that physical wealth is necessary. Although too often, many concern themselves with chasing physical riches, without first empowering themselves, with the proper knowledge of self, and taking care of one's physical health. So it's important to first get right with self, before seeking to possess the riches of the physical world. Now, one can understand why the info in this book is provided now, as opposed to the first two books.

The book will include segments of All You Need to Know to Become an Entrepreneur. The first Business Know How book I've written.

There is a saying which states, "A fool and their money will soon depart." I believe it goes something like that. The bottom line is that if you ask most people who have developed wealth and lost through business matters, they would tell you in so many words it was because of their lack of sound financial literacy, and their failure to do certain duties. Knowledge is the foundation, and without it one cannot obtain and maintain anything.

I believe the most important lesson, I've learned from

being an author and entrepreneur, is to not be scared to Start Over. Success isn't a straight line from where you start, to a finish line. In between, sometimes there are disappointments and setbacks. We're spirits having a physical experience. Yes, we're greater than most can imagine. Yet, we do tend to back track to old thinking. Even the best, do it. I'm at the point in will where I will get back up from any knock down. Hopefully, you're at this point in your awakening. Coming to this point, or making the concerted effort to reach this stage in your development.

Let's reflect on, what the first two books of Third Eye Awakening series taught us.

THOUGHTS

I try my best to keep up to date with what many financially successful people are saying. What many are stating is that the only way to get out the rat race is to invest in real estate, precious metals, commodities, or entrepreneurism.

It's quite obvious that being an author places me in a place to understand commodities, as an investment. 95% of my book sales are the result, of me printing and selling my titles straight to the customer. If I print 200 copies of a book, and set out to sell each at $10. It amounts to $2,000. Purchasing physical products for sale, gives you a sure idea as to what you'll earn. If you have 1,000 of an item and the price for each is $5. The earnings will amount to $5,000. With commodities the biggest concern is having, or creating an outlet to sell the products, and also having, or creating a customer base. Honestly, coming from the streets, and experiencing all that I've experienced, with learning about product awareness, sales, and building a customer base in that world, makes commodities my favorite investment route. It's one of the best routes I know to making money. For anyone who has sales skills, it's an easy way to build wealth. Even if they start off with a very small amount of capital. Now, if someone were to have a considerable amount of money to invest. The option of wholesaling to businesses is just as lucrative as selling retail to customers.

I'm a New Yorker born and raised. Having lived in Long Island most of my life. The two counties (Suffolk/Nassau) are amongst the most expensive communities to live within the U.S. Luckily, as an author, I've had the opportunity to travel a bit, and visit several cities and states. People, wherever they reside, need a place to lay their head. So real estate is also a great investment. When I lived in Texas I realized that the cost of living within many areas is about 30% to 50% of what it is within Long Island, and the boroughs of NYC. This makes real estate a very serious option for investing. Being a person who is always concerned about debt, I'm not a big fan of owing money, long length loan terms, or high interest rates. I believe that money borrowed, should be utilized to make more money. The reality is that all loans, mortgages accrue interest. Banks and lenders need to earn money. Otherwise they wouldn't lend money. The smart investor is always looking for an opportunity to maximize their ability to earn. The idea is to owe less, and earn more. Sacrifice on the front end, to reach pay off of loan quicker, so you can begin to earn, and profit. Real estate is a great way to develop residual income, and long-term income.

Precious metals, like gold and silver have always shown to mature in value over time. I myself have just started to invest in silver. One can invest in grade coins, or bullions. A bullion is gold or silver before being turned into a coin, the value is in weight. They're purchased in 1 oz. slabs and up. The value is purely determined by weight. Whereas the value of grade coins is determined by its rarity. Meaning, if there is a grade coin, where there are a 1,000 of them in circulation. It will have a value less than a grade coin, where there are only 50 of them which exist.

Toward my late teens into my early twenties I was blessed to come across such business books as, One

Minute Manager, 7 Habits of Highly Effective People and from there the search was on to figure out how I was going to put the pieces together and forge my destiny. So for all the teachers and writers throughout the ages who have manifested their thoughts and poured their energies out into the universe I'm grateful because, I've learned and felt all of your callings. There truly is magic within books.

My personal experiences are vast and many. From the school of hard knocks and the streets, to various jobs ranging from menial to supervising others I've had the ability and privilege to learn within many realms of life. If I had to mention one single person who has influenced or impressed upon me the most I would have to say Napoleon Hill. The Law of Success up to this very date has been the best work I've read detailing how to reprogram your Thinking, and readily prepare you to do what's going to allow you to be prosperous, in all areas of your life. His descriptive detail of how individuals like Henry Ford have become successful has convinced me beyond truth that there is a master plan in regards to obtaining success.

Put your thinking cap on and enjoy the ride. Third Eye Awakening III.

OWN YOUR OWN LIFE

Fall Down Seven Times, and Get Back Up Eight.

This Japanese proverb, for me explains life's struggles one faces to find their place through the travels of various ambitions to create a living for themselves. Whether, that be for personal, professional, or financial stature. As much as people are the same in many ways, they're also very different in the manner they choose to exist.

One of Our Greatest Tasks Is Not to Lose Our Humanity, In the Process of Failing and Falling.

It's a task to wholeheartedly accept the responsibility for whatever life brings our way. Even if it at times seems like we've been ambushed, betrayed, thwarted, or misled. But our life is our own to manage, and there's no one to place in charge of such responsibility. This is one of the qualities, which makes humans quite different than any other species. Our development in consciousness, allows us to be in partnership with the universe. The vision is being developed within each of us. As we are all charged with a specific task, and it's our duty to manifest this outside ourselves.

It's in Falling Down, That We Learn the Most about Ourselves, and Also the Way.

Many, would state that being in one's forties is still young. Yet, as I look back over my experiences. I'm reminded that when things were going perfect, I wasn't challenged. Honestly, I believe that comfortability has been problematic for me, because it's been through struggle and problems that I've grown the most, and done the most as well. Most of the skills I've developed for the most part have been the result of me acknowledging a wall I may of bumped into, or a failure as the result of not knowing, or doing something at the right time. Which basically boils down to a lack of knowing, because when you know better you do better. As the saying, goes.

All of the Religious Text Were Brought Fourth to Humans, to Give Instruction on How to Live and Obtain the Most Out of Oneself, Each Other and the Physical Plain.

The universe is expressing a vision which is unique to each of us. A vision, which is to determine the place and role we're to serve in the world. A position which is to bring joy, and fulfillment to ourselves, as individuals, and for the betterment of the world. Light is light, and a position or title, doesn't make one's good greater than another. No different than darkness is darkness, and a bad deed is a bad deed. Degrees, of good and bad, and such are deceptive, and caused by feelings in perception. It's not Truth. Truth, is life, and the progress and betterment of Life.

As a Child One Looks at People and Into the World, to Make the Choice as to Whom They Desire to Become.

Adults, wonder if they can become the person they want to be. Children, know for certain who they desire to become. They will tell you who it is they think serves an important role within the world. This, says a whole lot. Sometimes, the more we learn about the world, the more confused, we become about ourselves. It's imperative to learn the right knowledge. The right knowledge, is self fulfilling, and aides in the development of one's spiritual, and mental being. It will validate the goodness, and purpose within oneself. The right knowledge, sets the foundation for one's value system, in regards to self. Also, the value they see themselves serving others, and the world.

Have You Forgotten the Fearlessness of Your Youth?

Children haven't experienced, enough of the negative opinions of others to have self-doubt. They feel they're capable of doing anything, and if their lucky there's a network of adults who constantly reinforce this idea.

What happens to the adult who once was that child, or teen who possessed aspirations of building skyscrapers. Yet who has now become content with building one family houses? At what point in life do humans become prone to losing the steam and desire to not just be players, but also champions? This is very important to understand. One thing for certain. The American public-school system, is more influenced by politics, and economics than the concern to enlighten children, and young people with the knowledge they need to become productive, whole beings who are evolving, and who are consciously taking part in the process.

"As a Teen I Became a Member of the Nation of Gods & Earths, and it instilled in me a sense of self-worth, identity, and the need to grow. With the understanding that if I didn't take control of my mind, thoughts and actions. Then I would be nothing more than a slave of a mental death and power. One's life should mean more to them than just getting married, becoming a parent, getting up in the morning. Or any other time throughout the day, just to go to a job. Which brings them no joy. Then do the same thing over the next day, and the next day, 5 days a week. Is there more? Of course, there is. The United States is the number one world power economically and militarily. It's standing in education is ranked at fourteenth in the world when compared to 40 countries. The top ten ranked nations in education in order are Japan, Singapore, Hong Kong, Finland, United Kingdom, Canada, Netherlands, Ireland, and Poland. One has to wonder how can a nation who represents the greatest power in military might, exporting, importing goods, and financial standing, isn't at the top in education. Is this by mere coincidence, or a product of deliberate intent? I would say the public-school system prepares young people to go out into the world, and be employees. Unfortunately, they're not even taught to be great employees. If they're not imparted with the knowledge and skills to keep evolving as individuals, in career, and profession. Then it's impossible to become entrepreneurs, or private contractors. This requires a whole other level of thinking.

I would say in 2000 is when I seriously assessed my skills, qualities and life ambitions to see where to begin. At 28 years old, more than anything else I realized it was a late start. Yet, I knew that the roads I've traveled had prepared me to handle anything life threw my way. Most importantly, through the rough roads I accumulated an enormous amount of worthy skills, even if the knowledge of them weren't truly developed. When, I stared around at my peers around my age, it was evident that I was more developed. The pressure applied to the rock over many years manifests a diamond."

The Things We Do to Earn a Living, Manage Friendships, and Relationships Are the Result of Skills.

Skills, according to the dictionary mean. The ability to do something well.

The bottom line is whatever one does in life, translates into skills because without the know-how, nothing gets done. There's a saying, which goes that we all walk around with a tool box, and as we learn a skill we place it in the tool box. Yet, what most don't realize is that skills are transferrable, amongst settings, trades and platforms. Whether, one is selling a product in the streets, inside a store, at a stand, car dealer, or cable company the skill is sales, right. People work in a profession for X amount of years, and assume they can only be a good salesman, woman in that industry. Wrong, sales is a skill. So is product awareness. The only difference is one will be dealing with a different product, and customer base. The same way one learned about the product and customer base in the previous industry, requires the same amount of due diligence. Maybe even less of your time.

People Are Taught to Chase the Money Before They Even Find Themselves.

Money is man-made, it has no value outside the value that humans give it. All physical riches, and mans manifestations of nature, for various uses and purposes have value, because humans place a value. So, all of these things' humans develop. The question remains that since this is so. Why do humans place more value on things they create than their own lives? It's the car, house, motorcycle, furniture, technology, trinkets, and job or hustle you employ to get these things, more important than one's physical health, mind state, spiritual condition? Any sane person will think, No!"

Wouldn't it make sense that instead of Kindergarten to 12 grade children being taught and prepared to be good employees that they also be enlightened in regards to the development of their internal self (mind & spirit?) Each of us is unique, and it's not until we find ourselves, and our purpose, can we become truly useful to ourselves and the world. When you find yourself, then you'll also find your purpose. When you find your purpose, you'll find the path and lane in life which is meant for you. There's success to be found in living your truth. No one can do what is mean for you, better than you. Dogs are meant to bark. Cats are meant to meow, and each of us is meant to do our own thing. Whether, this translates into being a business owner, career or the arts is between you and the Universe.

SKILLS

Take inventory of your skills, your likes, dislikes, and what motivates you. All of these are fingers which are pointing to a certain pathway saying, "Go this way." Are you content with the life your living? Let's remove money from the equation. Many people think earning, and having a lot of money will solve their problems. This just isn't so. Many financially wealthy and famous people, and folks who have more money than one can spend in a lifetime have committed suicide, lived reckless lives, were drug and alcohol addicts, abusive to themselves and others. Guess what? Many people right now would give up their material wealth, just to be a more complete person, find, and do what inspires them.

You're with yourself twenty-four hours a day. In fact, it's no lie that you're with yourself more than anyone else you set your eyes upon, or know. Why be miserable by working a job, employing a skill set, or living a life that your eternal self, the being no one sees but you aren't satisfied with? It's senseless, you're with yourself twenty-four hours a day. So, make yourself happy. You'll make others happy too, by being happy with what you do. This translates into doing a skill well, or creating a product or service which is useful to others.

Let's get back to the money, which is also important. But, lets always remember Self comes first, then man made things. Be inspired to do something, in a great way, and be business minded so you can earn a good financial value, by doing what you do. Okay, let's move on......

The world of skills:

Soft Skills:

Adaptability
Problem Solver
Collaborator
Dependable
Time Management
Critical Thinking
Self-Confident
Handles Pressure Well
Creative
Great Verbal Communicator
Leadership
Team Builder
Patient

Hard Skills:

Word Processing
Proofreader
Technical Writing
Creative Writing
Sales
Consulting
Customer Service
Contract Review
Typing
Collections

Hard skills are the abilities which are learned through a classroom, online course, or other learning platforms. Soft skills, are considered people skills. The question remains which skill set is more important. Well, this all depends on the company, and the job market at the time. Companies with limited resources tend to prefer candidates with hard skills, because they don't need to be taught the specific task. Yet, many established companies prefer candidates with soft skills, because people skills are hard to be taught. It's what individuals learn naturally, by interacting with people and becoming better at the skill. These types of companies who prefer people with soft skills, feel they can always teach a candidate how to perform tasks. Whether the skill be typing, collections, carpentry, etc.

Most people mistake a trade with skills. Being a mechanic is a trade. The things you do as a mechanic are skills. An employer and job interviewer, are interested in your skill set, but too often resumes are filled with info specifically about the trade. When it's the skills which separate one tradesman/woman from the other. The more skills one possesses, the more valuable and marketable one is, for themselves and to an organization.

Let's take a look at some positions, and the difference in skill sets of the individuals:

John and Jason are both car wash attendants. They're the two best workers at the shop. The only difference between the two is John has great customer service and sales skills. He knows how to greet the customers, explain the services, and he also knows how to speak to the customer after the service is provided on the vehicle. So, he's a great opener and closer. His tips range from $150-$300 weekly. Whereas Jason earns roughly $80-$120 in tips weekly. They both do about the same number of vehicles each week, and earn 40% of service cost per vehicle. John earns about 95% more in tips than Jason due to; customer service, and sales skills.

Let's move on to another example:

Michelle and Jerome are both Quality Assurance Inspectors for an over the counter drug manufacturer. They both were hired the same day, and have been working for the company now 10 months. During this time Jerome has only worked on the production lines. While Michelle started on the production lines, and after sixty days, she asked the Quality Assurance Supervisor to be able to learn another area. Their supervisor was thrilled that she wanted to learn other areas of production, and she was then assigned to the encapsulation area. After another sixty days she was moved to the boxer area. This area is where pill bottles go through a conveyor belt, and placed one by one in boxer sleeves. The sleeves are imprinted by laser with a lot number, and expiration date.

Michelle, has been approached by the Production Manager, about being promoted to a Production Supervisor position. He cites that he's been observing her for the last three months, and likes how she's able to adapt to other areas, is very detail oriented with paperwork, gets along with workers in the area, takes responsibility for her work and is proactive with her career. The Production Supervisor position pays $6.00 more an hour. Michelle possessing the following skills made this happen; adaptability, detail oriented, great communicator, proactive.

One more example before moving on:

Josh and Sherman are sales consultants for an organization who provides health, property & casualty insurance. Both have been working with the same organization for two years. The first year Josh and Sherman earned around thirty-five thousand. The second year Josh earned forty thousand, and Sherman earned around fifty-five thousand. Both Josh and Sherman spend the first hour at the office cold calling potential clients. Then they hit the streets. Sherman is social media savvy, and belongs to three local civic organizations, as well as four chambers of commerce. He also attends all of his sons' school football games, whether at the school, or at the competitors. He makes it his business to introduce himself, and services to at least 5 new people at each game. Josh on the other hand doesn't utilize social media or belong to civic organizations. He relies solely on cold calling people he and wife personally know. Once in a while he'll attend local community events and prospect. Sherman, earned fifteen thousand dollars more than Josh by utilizing the following skills; social media, networking, community interaction.

BUILDING A CAREER

There's a process and system to building anything. Building a career is no different.

When one attends grade school, there were courses one needs to take and to fulfill our curriculum requirements. The same is required for those who attend universities. One cannot obtain an associates, bachelors or masters degree unless requirements are met. One cannot obtain a GED unless requirements are met. Every aspect of school is based on a planned curriculum.

If one would like to reach a certain level career wise, and earnings within their profession which is considerably above what those earn at an entry level position. Then it's necessary to have some type of plan to build upon skills, and know what routes to take in their career to advance.

"When, I started working as a Quality Assurance Inspector, the first company was an over the counter drug manufacturer. After four months of working there, I could have easily gone on to become a Production Supervisor, earn more, and be given a bit more responsibility. I realized though that as a Quality Assurance Inspector it provided me with the opportunity to learn the whole packaging process. An opportunity which is limited on the Production Supervisor side. The production side is more concerned with the numbers, and producing. Quality Assurance, is concerned with quality, creating and ensuring effective processes exist, and are carried out from start to finish.

As time went by I realized that the more I learned about operations the more valuable and marketable I would be to myself, and an organization. So, I sacrificed earning more money to obtain knowledge. Which to me represents a necessary trade off, most high achievers must make at some point in their career.

After working for three companies as a Quality Assurance Inspector, I landed the opportunity with Natures Bounty (NBTY.) My first role was a Quality Assurance Inspector in the gel cap production area. It was actually a building all on its own. I know my next move had to be an upward move, so I looked around and took inventory of available positions. There weren't any. There was Production Lead, which the position basically earned just a little more than I was currently earning. Then there was one Production Supervisor per shift.

Five months after being employed as a Quality Assurance Inspector a position opened up in one of the packaging buildings. I jumped right on it. Three months later a Production Supervisor position became available and I applied. It took about two weeks to receive a response. To my surprise, one day the Assistant Manager approached me to let me know I obtained the position, and that he'd be my new supervisor. He mentioned I beat out about 17 to 20 applicants. Some of whom have worked for the company for several years. The reason I was chosen, he cited is due to skills, and being a better long-term investment for the organization.

As a Quality Assurance Inspector, I became well informed of processes, and being able to pay attention to detail. Now, as a Production Supervisor I was learning leadership skills, and how to deal with people as individuals and employees, from disciplining to encouraging."

It wasn't by chance that I beat out all of them candidates. I purposely developed the necessary skills to obtain the position, and was rewarded without second guesses. We must be conscious in our decisions, and moves to build a career just like we're conscious to go grocery shopping. In your mind you already have figured out what's going to take place, and how you're going to get there. Well, it's the same here.

Let's play a scenario:

Lisa is a cashier at a very large merchandise chain retail store. She's been working for the organization for thirteen months now, and has a GED. Her desire is to be a store manager. There's only one store manager for each shift. The company protocol for hiring store managers, is that they either have at least an associate's degree, or three years working in a retail environment. But, the company started an in-house six-month management training program, to train and promote those who don't meet the other criteria, but are already employees. Since Lisa doesn't have an associate's degree, and has never worked in a retail environment outside of the current job, her only option is to enroll within the companies in house management training program. She enrolls, and six months later becomes a manager. Her promotion didn't happen by chance. Lisa evaluated her situation, along with her goal. Then she took inventor of the pros and cons of her present status, made decisions and proactively took the necessary steps to accomplish what she sought.

GETTING BACK UP AFTER FALLING DOWN

Fall Down Seven Times, Get Back Up Eight.

In today's economic and business climate where so much outside factors effects ones current and future employment status, uncertainty is what many deal with. What happens when one does take a fall? Whether they lose their job, their company goes out of business, or their earnings are drastically cut down in size. How does one come back after starting all over?

If You Did It Once You Can Do It Again.

It's easy to get in the mind state of feeling sorry for oneself. Yet, this does nothing but delay the process of getting back to Now. What happened yesterday last week, last month, is the past. Always focus on the present, and the present is Now. Everything is a part of a process, and so rebuilding is a process. Many people find themselves having to start all over in professions which are outside of their normal careers. In doing so they may be beginning at entry level positions, and their earnings are quite bit lower than their normal pay. This can be a blow to one's ego. On the flip side it can also be the drive to make a committed decision to build a new career, and reach a level they're comfortable with financially.

"One of the most challenging things I did was leave a

promising career in management to start my own publishing company. In 2005 I established Third Eye Publishing. It would have been impossible had I not brought with me the skills I learned within the streets, and the extra ones I developed as a Quality Assurance Inspector, and Production Supervisor. In the streets I learned how to negotiate, customer service, sales team development, leadership, and as a Quality Assurance Inspector and Production Supervisor I learned processes, standards of operation, how to be more effective at leadership and building employees, processes, and working with the many people necessary to add their skills, and work to a project, and organization. Within six months of releasing Love Don't Live Here revised edition in Nov 2005, I would go on to sell close to 5,000 copies within the NYC and Long Island street market alone. From there I negotiated a deal with a distributor, to distribute the title to the chain retail book store market (Borders, Waldenbooks, Barnes & Nobel, B.Dalton.) Learning how to leverage skills from one platform to another, and being adaptable is how I was able to make things happen.

What had become even more challenging for me, and a true test of my skills, was when the publishing industry began to go through drastic changes due to the EBook invention, and technological advancements in the industry, along with the recession of 2008 and 2009. My distributor closed its doors, as did many distributors, book stores, and even publishers who were put out of business due to books being within the warehouses of distributors who filed bankruptcy. I would wind up going through a contractual disagreement with the company who picked up the publisher contracts, a sister company of the company I was in contractual relations with. This basically put my company operations in a stalemate for one year. Finally, after going through an arbitrator and settling things, I broke ties with them. I realized I would need to restructure, and rethink things. Therefore, I decided to take a hiatus. Since it was evident to me technology had become an important part of operations on every level, I figured I would keep my social media pages active, while I take the time to become social media savvy, and learn to integrate, secure data and become more technological equipped. Failure is a part of success. It's also a part of the learning curve. Its where we come to the awareness that what we currently know isn't quite good enough, and that we must equip ourselves with more knowledge."

Pick Yourself Up.

There's really no other choice in the matter, but to pick yourself up and start all over again. We're here to live this life, whether we strive to live it to the fullest or not. In other words, if we don't strive to do better, we deprive ourselves of the goodness of existing, which comes from challenging ourselves to be better, by doing better. The man, or woman who has the ability to play professional basketball, and yet chooses to stay at semi pro level, because they don't want to give a little more effort, and go harder is robbing themselves of the experience the next level will give them with opening more doors, and opportunities to grow as a person.

Think Positive, But Also Be a Soldier.

Fight for your life. Utopia is a human idea society reaches for. Yet, you as an individual must deal with reality, or be a failure. The reality is that since childhood many of the obstacles one faces are external. They're societal ills, and the result of ill thinking and actions, of other humans. We must become stronger than our own doubts, strengthen our shortcomings, be defiant in the face of opposition and obstacles. Positive Thinking is useless without also the knowledge of the reality that we're all in one way affected by the thoughts and actions of others. In picking ourselves up, we must take responsibility for our own thoughts and actions which brought the fall. Yet, we must also acknowledge the external factors, and develop the know how to go over, sidestep and become immune to outside attack. It's in many ways the same path an organization, or nation makes itself in penetrable to outside forces.

Falling down gives you insight into where you stand in life and also what you're made of. It's also a chance to be honest with yourself about your shortcomings. At this point a wise thing to do is evaluate your skills, and the things you can build upon to make you a stronger person. There's no one pathway to success, and so now you have the chance to review options. You can possibly use this time to obtain training or education of a new career, or business.

"In my case, when I stopped publishing under Third Eye Publishing right away I made the decision to both, learn a new skill, and also build upon existing ones. Feeling a little burnt out I also decided it was the perfect time to take a step back from the grind, hustle, and get more into self. In doing this, over time I began to think dearly about events which led up to everything, and also what were my future plans. One thing I knew I needed to do now more than ever is humble myself. It was necessary that I made some sacrifices because, my income was going to be considerably lower than I became accustomed to. In fact, I was honest with myself that it would be this way for at least five years. I mentally prepared myself to get in hustler mode as if I was starting my career life all over. In essence I was though. A new path is always best to be looked at with fresh eyes.

After the notorious September 11th attack of the Twin Towers in NYC, many people lost their jobs due to industries being affected. When the mortgage crisis hit causing the recession, another wave of financial doom lingered. Many people through these events found themselves having to readjust, or completely start over. Unfortunately, there's a segment of the population who never recovered. Some could not make the transition to find other careers. Others refused to take jobs which were below their skill set, and normal earnings. Getting back up after the fall is never easy, and it requires a lot of spiritual, mental toughness, discipline, and a plan to get back on track."

Entrepreneurship & investing are the only two routes for one to take to get out of the rat race. Warren Buffet, the billionaire, philanthropist and investor states one has to find a way to earn money while they're sleeping. Otherwise they'll be working for the rest of their life. The next section is going to be dedicated to the different types of business structures, so those interested in starting a business can get a better understanding of the pros and cons of each set up. In today's technological world opportunities are endless, even while one is holding down a 9to5 and career. There are twenty-four hours in a day, and it's not a second more for anyone, no matter how wealthy and successful they are. Therefore, it basically comes down to you as an individual, and what you do.

BASIC TYPES OF BUSINESS STRUCTURES

A. Sole Proprietorship.

A sole proprietorship is a business owned by one individual, and it is not incorporated. It is the easiest business structure to establish, but it provides the least amount of protection to the owner. All business liabilities become the owner's personal liabilities. All income and expenses of the business are placed on the owner's personal income tax return. As a sole proprietor, the owner may be liable for income taxes, self-employment taxes, Social Security, and Medicare taxes (FICA).

Disadvantages:

1. The owner is personally liable for all business's debts, and liability is not limited to the value of the business. The owner is personally liable for any and all debt incurred.
2. It is usually more difficult to borrow money or obtain outside investment with a sole proprietorship than with other types of business structures.
3. If the owner becomes ill for any reason, the business is likely to fail.
4. All management responsibility is with the owner.

Establishing a Sole Proprietorship:

In order to establish a sole proprietorship, the owner should:

1. Obtain local business licenses.
2. Check on local zoning ordinances, regulations, and other land use restrictions.

3. Determine if your particular business requires a state license to operate. Find out if any federal permits or licenses are required.
4. File with your appropriate county official for the business name, then file an affidavit of publication. These guidelines apply to almost all states. Please check with your county clerk to make sure you are adhering to your states rules.
5. Locate a good insurance agent to obtain fire, accident, liability, and theft insurance. You may operate your business out of your home and have no employees. Yet there is a possibility that a fire occurs, or some of your property is stolen. So, when making the decision as to whether or not you need insurance and how much that you're going to need take your time to think things through and take everything into account.
6. Obtain an accountant. All profits and losses from the business are to be reported on your personal income tax.

When you file the paperwork with the county clerk to conduct business under any name other than your own, your business becomes known as, for example, John Smith d/b/a (doing business as) Acme Plumbing. You must file paperwork to obtain a d/b/a name if you wish to open a bank account under any name other than your own.

B. Partnership
A general partnership is similar to doing business

as a sole proprietor except there are more than one owner has partners with whom to share the business's losses and gains. The owners do not have the same liability protection as with a corporation or limited liability company, but a partnership is a fast way to get a business started.

Advantages:
1. Partnerships are basically as easy to establish as sole proprietorships.
2. The profits from the business flow directly through to the partners personal tax returns.
3. You don't have to register with your state and pay a fee, as you do to establish a corporation or limited liability company.

Disadvantages:
1. Partnerships may have different business objectives and visions.
2. Business debts and liabilities the partners are personally liable for.
3. Each partner's commitments to the business may not be equal.
4. Personal quarrels may occur.

Establishing a Partnership:
In order to establish a partnership, the owners should:
1. Obtain local business licenses.
2. Check on local zoning ordinances, regulations, and other land use restrictions.

3. Determine if your particular business requires a state license to operate. Find out if any federal permits or licenses are required.
4. File with your appropriate county official for the business name, then file an affidavit of publication. These guidelines apply to almost all states. Please check with your county clerk to make sure you are adhering to your states rules.
5. Get an EIN Employee Identification Number from IRS using form SS-4.
6. Draft written agreement between the partners determining a financial plan, management responsibilities, day to day activities, etc.
7. Locate a good insurance agent to obtain fire, accident, liability, and theft insurance. You may operate your business out of your home and have no employees. Yet there is a possibility that a fire occurs, or some of your property is stolen. So when making the decision as to whether or not you need insurance and how much that you you're your time to think things through and take everything into account.
8. Obtain an accountant. All profits and losses from the business are to be reported on your personal income tax.

When you file the paperwork with the county clerk to conduct business under any name other than your own, your business becomes known as, for example, John Smith d/b/a (doing business as) Acme Plumbing. You must file paperwork to obtain a d/b/a name if you wish to open a bank account under any name other than your own.

C. S Corporation

An S Corp is a special type of corporation, of particular interest to sole proprietorships or partners. An entrepreneur who is interested in incorporating his or her business to limit personal liability assets may choose to do so through an S Corp. The S Corp allows the entrepreneur to protect his or her assets in the event of business failure. A simple sole proprietorship or partnership does not provide this protection.

Advantages:
1. The S corporation has shareholders and is taxed like a sole proprietorship or partnership.
2. The owner has the protection of limited liability without having to pay corporate taxes.
3. The corporation is a separate legal entity. This means a corporation can open a bank account, own property, and do business under the corporation's name, protecting the owner's personal name.
4. Earnings of an S Corporation—after paying a reasonable salary to the shareholders—can be passed through as distributions of profits, and are not subject to self-employment taxes.

Disadvantages:
1. S Corps are not treated the same in every state. In some states an S Corp is treated like any other corporation regarding tax liability. It is important to seek professional advice before

committing to set up an S corp. I placed this in the disadvantage area because S Corps in general are not the same size companies as C Corps which are publicly traded and revenue is much greater.

2. There are restrictions on who can be owners (shareholders) of an S Corporation. An S Corporation can have no more than seventy-five shareholders, and none of the shareholders can be non-resident aliens. Also, shareholders cannot be other corporations or LLCs.

Establishing an S Corp:

To form an S Corp you must file articles of incorporation with the Secretary of State. An S Corp is formed by filing incorporation documents with your state's department of state, department of corporations, or other appropriate department. Once the business has incorporated, the owners may decide to file taxes as an S Corporation.

D. Limited Liability Company (LLC)

An LLC is a type of company, authorized to exist only in certain states, whose owners and managers receive the limited liability and (usually) tax benefits of an S Corporation without having to conform to the S Corporation restrictions.

Advantages:

1. The LLC allows for multiple owners or members. Additionally, there is a managing member who also enjoys the rewards of limited liability, and is typically the person responsible

for managing the business.

2. The profits or losses of the business pass directly through to the owner's personal income tax return on Form 1040. The LLC files a Form 1065, and then lists each member's taxable profit on Form K-1. In other words, the LLC does not file taxes.

3. An LLC offers greater flexibility in ownership and ease of operation. The owners of an LLC can distribute profits in any manner they see fit. For example, you and a partner are owners of an LLC. Your partner contributed forty thousand dollars for capital. You only contributed ten thousand dollars, but you perform 90 percent of the work. The two of you decide that, in the interest of fairness, you will split the profits evenly, meaning you will get 50 percent and your partner will receive 50 percent. This is possible to do with an LLC, whereas other business structures do not allow such flexibility.

Disadvantages:

1. Earnings of most members are generally subject to self-employment tax. There are other disadvantages that should be researched. LLC is the newest of all the business structures, so you will need an experienced tax professional to explain all its details.

2. There is not one guideline which governs how Limited Liability Companies operate within all states. So if an LLC conducts business within many states there is a possibility it may not

receive the same treatment.

3. Conversion of an existing business to LLC company status could result in tax recognition on appreciated assets.

4. Not all businesses can be formed as an LLC. Businesses in trust and insurance and banking are in most instances prohibited from forming an LLC.

5. In California, accountants, architects, lawyers, doctors and other licensed healthcare professionals are restricted from forming their business as a LLC.

Establishing an LLC:

1. Choose an available business name.

2. File articles of organization and pay filing fee which can range anywhere from $100 to $800.

3. Obtain any licenses and permits your business needs. The licenses all depend on the type of business you're starting.

4. Publish your notice of intent to form an LLC (this is only required within a few states). Check

5. Check with your accountant, attorney or the business organization that you're seeking to assist you with forming your LLC.

There are several business savvy websites like legalzoom.com, limitedliabilitycompanycenter.com, sba.gov, nolo.com, irs.gov, incorporate.com and bizfiling.com so get on your pc and get going. There is a saying which is so true, "A man who fails plan plans to fail"

THINK ON THIS

Build a Foundation upon Knowledge

Educate yourself about the things you need to know, and the things which interest you.

This is your foundation.

Focus on What Matters

It's true that with experience comes wisdom.

Focus on What Matters is one of the most important lessons, one can learn. For many people waste time where it need not be spent.

Prioritize priorities, and give little time to that which needs little time given to.

What Matters Most, is where you should dedicate most of your time.

Self-Mastery

Obtaining Knowledge of Self isn't obtained through reading books, or doctrines alone. It's a process of learning that which pertains to self, and letting go of that which is holding us back of becoming, more complete and a better version of ourselves.

Find Your Purpose

If you don't find your purpose, nothing else matters.

Begin with the End in Mind

Sometimes the destination can be a zigzag path, around and around in circles. Or it may seem like a hike up a steep hill. Yet if you know where you're going, it doesn't matter how you get there. It's all about whether you're tough enough to accomplish the task.

Focus on Business

Whatever your business is focus on it, and on the thoughts and activities which will enable you to establish and grow it.

Success, isn't the end of the road, and there will always be cycles. Failure isn't permanent, and perseverance is the friend of all those who witness their dreams.

The Fall

The fall is one of the most important things which will ever happen to you in life. If you're extremely ambitious, you will have, or will fall at least once.

It's the lessons, you take from your situation, yourself, and people, which will determine the rest of your life. Do you move on? Or do you seek to play it safe for now on? Maybe you just fall to pieces.

Find Yourself First

Everything isn't for everyone. If you don't know yourself, find yourself. Don't chase money, chase what inspires you. Happiness is the journey. Happy people never reach a destination.

Simplify Your Life

Simplify your life, by cutting out the riff raff and unnecessary.

This goes for yourself, people and situations.

Take Notes

There's no better teacher than life itself. Oh, and let's add books to the equation.

Pay attention, and take notes. Your life depends on it.

Humans Are Their Own Enemies

Humans are the only enemy's mankind faces. All of the turmoil, wars, and human suffering outside of natural catastrophes, is the result of humans.

Life is But a Dream

The human mind is a tool humans utilize to conceive the realities of the Eternal Mind. Life is but a Dream. The magic, of transforming mental energy in the use of physical matter, shaped in the forms of various tools, for the use of pleasures, and to make human life more bearable.

Be Strengthened by Your Struggles

It's no doubt about it that we are defined more by our struggles, and adversities than anything else.

Those who know the truth, are those who live it. Textbook theory is great. But experience just brings a whole other level of understanding. When you've travelled the many roads of success, mishaps, and missteps, it matures you in a way that would not happen, on your own.

The process of rebuilding, at times is daunting but at the same time inspiring because, you know it's on you. Do you let others get in your way with their mediocre nonsense? Do you fall victim to emotional attachments, which serve to benefit others, at your expense? Or do you have that focus and blindness, to see only what's important and necessary to get the job done?

The choice is always our own.

Communication Is an Art

Communication is an art. There're ways to say what you want without saying one word. You do it unconsciously whether you know it or not.

Most people miss out on what people are really saying by focusing on words only.

Commit Yourself

Talent is great. But no matter how good you are, you have to be committed to getting better, by learning and applying your skills. You have to write, sing, rap, perform, and practice what you do constantly. As well as study the theory of your craft.

Grow Your Inventory

Grow your customer & distribution base.

Inventory sitting around is money wasted. Evaluate what sells, and doesn't. Buy more of what sells, than what doesn't.

Calculated Risks

All actions should be a calculated risk. Think before you act, and never be in a rush. Gather the facts before action.

The Steps

There's a process and steps to a goal. Work the steps, as tiresome as they may seem. The building process is necessary.

Intelligence Created the Mountain

There's one source of intelligence, which flows through all of the world's creations, and all plains of energy. This source, created the mountain, and is the mountain (problems, dilemmas.) Problems created are solvable by You because, intelligence created You.

Intelligence is within You, and therefore, is You. Point blank.

Know Your Focus

If you don't know your focus in life, then you don't know where you're at, or where you're going. You'll be doing any and everything, and dealing with everyone. If you know yourself, then you also know who to deal with, and who not to deal with, according to your life plan.

Love yourself because it's the hardest thing one will do. Doesn't make sense to love things, or this world, and other people, if you don't have self-love.

What's outside is within

To Know Thyself, is the first stage in viewing the world outside as a reflection, of what's within.

Build Your Goals around Your Life

Build your program around your personal style. Everyone has a personal style. One can only be the best at being themselves.

There's Struggles on Different Levels

Some people face their struggles, and some don't Point blank.

Everyone takes missteps, has falls, and everyone also has a next level. There's always going to be a struggle. Nothing remains the same. Things change, for the better, or worse.

The goal is to find balance, in all areas of your life. Love your life. You have to always work on your life. Never get into someone else, and forget about you. It's better to be by yourself, to build yourself, before companionship. No one can make you, and no one can rescue, you from yourself, and no one can find you, but you.

Everything Isn't for Everyone

You have to know what's for you, and what isn't. Every opportunity, isn't one which is in your best interest, according to your life design.

Put the Work In

1. Gotta put the work in, then talk about it.
2. It stops jealous folks from trying to interrupt your plans. So, get it done, then market. If it's not done, be very vague, and keep important

details to yourself, until it's done. Don't let your mind, play tricks on you. Get it done.